SOLDIER
SAVED BY OTHERS

EUGENE J. KAELIN

SOLDIER
SAVED BY OTHERS

PALMETTO
PUBLISHING
Charleston, SC
www.PalmettoPublishing.com

Copyright © 2023 by Eugene J. Kaelin

All rights reserved
No portion of this book may be reproduced, stored in a retrieval system, or transmitted in any form by any means–electronic, mechanical, photocopy, recording, or other–except for brief quotations in printed reviews, without prior permission of the author.

Paperback ISBN: 979-8-8229-2739-1
eBook ISBN: 979-8-8229-2740-7

TABLE OF CONTENTS

Chapter 1: Feelings	1
Adore…	2
Messes	2
Were Ashes, Now None	3
The Ordinary	3
Peace	4
Approved	4
Dream	5
Calmness	5
My Mother	6
Peace	6
Suddenly	7
Endless Space	7
Say Sorry	8
Love	8
Empathy	9
Free	9
Whimsical	10
Chapter 2: Rest	11
Holy	12
Into Sleep	12

Strife	12
Gratitude	13
Sweet Sleep	13
It Too Shall Pass	14
Worry	14
Kept	15
Guilt and Condemnation	15
The Living Rock	16
Ponder	16
Can It Be?	17
Respect	17
Full Decision	18
Calm	18
Chapter 3: Self	19
Children	20
Me	20
Much Belonging	20
Great Peace	21
Just Be	21
Faithful	22
Burdens	22
The Riddle	23
Grateful Heart	23

Drifting Away	24
Making It	24
Silence	25
Civility	25
Righteousness	26

Chapter 4: Dream — 27

Permanence	28
You Be You.	28
Heaven Itself	28
Christmas Now	29
Stars	29
Newness	29
Perfection	30
A Solace Prayer	30
Fear Not	31
Insist	31
Care	31
Solemn Vow	32
To Carry	32
Dream Again	33

Chapter 5: Religion — 35

A Religion	36

Holy Spirit	36
Forgiving Self	37
Jesus Letter	37
The World	38
As We Forgive	38
I Am Forgiven.	39
God's Love	39
Saved	40
Inheritance	40
Confidence	40
The Dark	41
A Process	41
Acknowledgements	43

Chapter 1
Feelings

Adore...

My worship of you has not been in vain. Even though you may not know how much I love you… I keep in retrospect our relationship and bless each day we are together, for you truly are a wonderful being. Maybe I only see it in adoration. But I believe you are worthy of it. For we were created for love, and love is the final say. Of things really hoped for, because we were created by love, we know and believe in love.

Messes

It can be naughty when you are having fun. The turn-on for you maybe not the same as others. Only maybe for you, what can be done with your thoughts? Never be ashamed, but try to fulfill, to be happy. Great joy is given to those who totally adapt to all changes.

Were Ashes, Now None

I took a step
Into the unknow
And found acceptance
Where there was none before.
I am truly alive now.
With the forgiveness of others,
Awake to do a good bidding of
The one who created me,
I go forward to rekindle a heart of fire,
Burning for good rather than for evil.
I feel cleansed and stepping out from the ashes.
Eugene Kaelin, Graduating CORE Veteran

The Ordinary

Blessings do flow and appear. Especially when were free. No more anxiety or fear. For our souls just must be. The brain must rest at times. Our bodies do also. But the universe gives us signs.

To every sister and brother, all our lives will complete in the end. The stories are all told. Grace will always send a victory courageous and bold.

Peace

Be compassionate and stable. Planted among the cypress. All can be able. We tend to be glorious. Tending to one another for life is never ending. We are all sisters and brothers in a world that is ever changing kindness and love as a guide. Will keep our hearts quiet and soft. Our minds open will always try and shall give truth and life.

Approved

You have been approved whole and holy. The word has been spoken to you. Believe and be saved. You have become what is true. Go out and love as you should. Much does need to be done. But the battle is already won. So relax and remember that you are loved always, forever.

Dream

A spark inside the mind and given into the soul. Alive and meaningful, seen from the heart. Spiritually blessed by a prayer, praised by grace. Still standing, because if we can think of it, we can do it. For the victory is always ours, for we are helped, not standing alone. Sunrises on us all, so hold on and trust, for before we were born, God knew. Remember you have been appointed, and God qualifies you as you go.

Calmness

The serene mind can become wiser and knowing. Think how special you are, and your thoughts will become calm. Remember the loving times when you shared loved from yourself to others. No one can share love without first loving oneself. The calm mind will always return love. Peace brings love, and love brings happiness and joy. Be at peace.

My Mother

She was a guide and kept me calm. Told me to not hide, prevented much harm. Allowed only good. Home was always safe. Gave what she could. Marched me at a good pace. Never did she falter to show me the good. Respected my father, always loved and always would. My Mother made it clear she would not always be near. So, because of her help. I kept her love so dear.

Peace

It is calm among the saintly egos. All is well with the lower and upper halves. Together they be in harmony. Going nowhere except to be. Enlisted in the army of contentment. Blowing the breeze with each other and remaining calm. The calmness of the summer tranquil sky, and both of us indulge in a quiet sigh.

Suddenly

Today is the first day. That you will see changes appear in your mindset. You will jump with glee, although much has been. It shall pass by, and what will become new again. For there shall be another side. Glory to glory, the universe unfolds. You are part of it. Much has been said. Relax and see you're a puzzle that fits.

Endless Space

Look beyond the present moment. See more of what can be imagined. For our time together shall end soon, and we shall never be here again. Grasp the precious life enfolding. Know who you really are now. A soul destined for much glory. A soul fully redeemed, and heaven bound. Be thankful for the opportunity. To solve the greatest mystery, we are all one in spirit even though we are not of same mind.

Say Sorry

I stepped on your toes; I'm sorry. I hurt your heart and mind. I'm sorry I got on your back; I'm sorry. I said something bad in gossip; I'm sorry. I thought badly about you; I'm sorry. Is my apology accepted? Or did it fall on deaf ears? I really do not care; at least I said I'm sorry.

Love

In the height of love, ecstasy does prevail. Attraction of self to others becomes more important. Love is determined by one's own feelings from mind. It is good to love and to be loved. Even when it becomes hurtful. Because it is better to love than to never have loved. Love is the only emotion from the heart that will finally prevail. For love conquers all. There is faith, hope, and love. The greatest is love.

Empathy

To care for another helps all concerned. For we need each other to survive. The species cannot go on unless we come together. So let us think only of others. When we do, we clearly see the task before us. To elevate our experiences with each other and to solve the problems that the world is having. For it is up to us; we are it. There is no-one else to consider than each other.

Free

Only the butterflies are free. We humans are trapped by our own designs, the mental bullying that becomes in us, which sometimes is from others. Even religion thoughts can enslave us. Shame and guilt become the main culprits; either we are bad or our actions are bad. Stay in focus; we all do bad things. We only need forgiveness and love.

Whimsical

You are here; I am their companion. Together we all are beings, maybe lost, but given the same end.

Compassion is worn on our sleeve. All looking for the same thing. Working hard to get it. But it takes real courage to succeed at the very best. It is in the trying that we follow and in the failures that we learn. After all is said and done, the judgments are really not ours at all and do not matter.

Chapter 2
Rest

Holy

We all are superstars. Hope and love is never ending. We are not separate; all have the Holy Spirt within. We are all one. Stop judging others; stop judging yourself. Be kind to the unkind. Be faithful to the unfaithful. For your basic nature is kindness and love. We are all holy from a holy given grace.

Into Sleep

Tend to doze when completely tired. The eyes become weighted, and the muscles start to ease. Great peace comes to mind, and phantoms may appear. As a drifting motion becomes very clear. Though it happens to all, we seem to believe that only our being is transformed to sleep and alone we dream.
New Years Eve 2022

Strife

The main thing is to keep your peace. Do not get angry, for it leads to strife. Help one another and stay loving. For hatred does end up killing the good. Stay joyful always, even though it gets rough. Joy is a gift from heaven. Receive it with loving kindness, and then you will be able to accept everyone in love.

Gratitude

How did I get here? Cannot really know, but
it all fell into place. Even when the walls
surrounded me. Free now to do good bidding.
For confidence now reigns and my trust in self.
Thank God for all his blessings.

Sweet Sleep

Holding you next to me. I can tell we are in love;
together we dwell in our closeness, sleeping with
each other amongst the starry nightfall. Blessed
toward each one emotions and not knowing any harm
given. Just a cuddle of love that is now totally given.

It Too Shall Pass

I am younger now than I was before. I was older than younger than that now all because of you. Your beauty far surpasses my imagination. You have become for me a super precious gift; my gratitude is never ending, and my reality now is blessed. True, life itself is more than possessing, but more in appreciation, our daily gifts, and you are for me a most wonderful presence.

Worry

Habits are hard to break, and much has been fought. It is never too late; the moment is all that we sought. Here we are from the past. So it really matters; much does fully last. How are egos flatter. There is no need to compare. As we journey forward, we climb up the many stairs to find that the light has always been for us.

Kept

No matter the circumstances or the situations, it is always becoming new, for the future does arrive. Evening to morn, dusk until dawn. It all evolves onward, no matter what happens; even ourselves become again something new. As progress goes forward and we still become. Something new and constantly changing as it all comes together. So massive the world of life, and thus we are.

Guilt and Condemnation

When the fear arrives with guilt that condemns, with guilt that condemns, remember to go through the struggle, and do not give up. Until the battle is won. It is not easy. The trial may last, but the adversity will teach a lesson in the end. A lesson of compassion. Where many others struggle together, we arrive; even though you feel alone, you are not. We all have some fear.

The Living Rock

We stand on a rock while sand underneath shifts; our peace us altered only from fear. The battle is won when we relax the fear. Contradictions of thought may come out of mind. The sense of it all is never always clear. But the selfless acts of sacrifice are in front of us. Today becomes a past memory. The grief is gone as we move on toward our events. We conquered all when we stood in quietness. We become what we were meant to be.

Ponder

To wonder why happens to many. Existence does present the facts. Only to be seen by just a few. While others close off their minds to grasp onto many falsehoods. The truths will sometimes be hidden and may seem to be buried. But it is there to be realized, given to the mind, presented mentally to us all.

Can It Be?
We came from bliss. We live in bliss. We shall die into bliss. What else can it be? This miracle of life can only be seen with heart and mind open. With arms and soul given. To each other in love, and then life itself becomes the treasure that it always was.

Respect
Understanding that life is not a commodity. To be used for self-interest. But life is a favor given, than received and given back to one another. Instead of taken and then stolen. Belonging requires a reception, not a rejection, and the only thing to reject is hatred. And the only emotion to respond to is love.

Full Decision

Tarry not for the good, but remain in the spirit. Much has been given; we are totally yours in the present. Wrapped up in the conclusion. Nothing has come from it, even with the adversity; remember that from it all we still go on eternally. Best to not hate yourself. I could have been different; maybe also you. But it had to be because of the power foretold. Remember the good given for even from the evil. It has all been a lesson learned from long ago.

Calm

Remain and try to be at one with your spirit. We can see what's above but must join up with what's within. The heart has many treasures, especially love that binds keep in perfect love. Your eternal life for us was created for this. And love does not require anything. Just the courage and work to survive the test. So whatever we think we deserve, remember that it's all very good with love.

Chapter 3
Self

Children

The little child, so mild and good, teaches the adult more than they know, for the little child can only bring its innocence to them if they listen. While the adult has only the experience which does hinder the thoughts of understanding and keeps the adult from their youthful selves. Children do bring grace.

Me

No one knows the real me. Who am I? The me who hates others' faults and cannot admit my own. It is not easy to be me. Even though I see me. I may be a me, but so are you. Me a mystic beyond myself and me above the hurt I inflict on me.

Much Belonging

The peace which is a given can only be taken when peace is received by us. It comes from nowhere and belongs in our minds. Which keeps it for us with a tranquil emotion. Where peace resounds among us. Keep the peace, for without it you may be perilous instead of a whole being kept in the warmth of great love.

Great Peace

When the savior was born on this Christmas day, salvation came to us humans, and peace was given unto our hearts. Though much strife does appear—just see the good many have done. Then you will see that peace has survived even with bad times.

Just Be

We are trying to live perfect lives within an imperfect world. Be who God created you to be, which is just yourself. An evolving human being who is special and unique like everyone else. Have a grateful heart for being part of the puzzle. For this life is either a miracle or not. But remember you were alive in it.

Faithful

The only time our life becomes accomplished is through faithfulness. Being faithful to self as well as others. We do not choose faithfulness. It comes by grace given from one who is faithful, our God. There is no answer to all the questions; we either do or die. The will of man is sometimes lazy. But from faith we crossed the finish line.

Burdens

Carry your cross; it bears your name. Though it is heavy on your shoulder. It has never been just a game, and we all are getting older. We shall know what comes from all of this. As moments and time keep passing on. The point of it all shall not be missed. For we are everlasting.

The Riddle

May we honor the dignity within and keep the love given. From the beginning to now. Nothing is lost when forgiveness reigns. From solitude we accept grace. Finally rescued and favored to be again the great people that we all are meant to be. Generous and good, compassionate and loving. Sisters and brothers belonging to one family of God.

Grateful Heart

Are we together on this? Do we have thankful hearts? Can gratitude overwhelm us? We breathe in, we breathe out. Our hearts onward are still beating. Our senses make us believe in ourselves. Our thoughts become many images. Life is given a miracle as is given and continues for us. Are we grateful?

Drifting Away

We can think together about sandy beaches and being with each other. Drinking rum every night and see what the sunset teaches. Maybe were broke, my mama. But I hear your voice so sweet. Talk to me, mama; make my life complete. Pardon me; my mind is on you. Can we drift to martini bay? We'll just close our eyes and come what may.

Making It

The act that contributes to success comes out of faith. Never does success only come on a lone act. It must resonate to include all involved in its making. Only when success evolves from an inspired thought that becomes real in a certain time it will exist. Exist only when conquered by faith. Faith that is given and received.

Silence

In the silence of our hearts, we hear the small voice permeating, telling of the goodness about to happen. We wait in anticipation for our hope to be strong. Many of us belong to the cooperative love which gains in popular belief. Even in all the turmoil which this world sometimes brings. We shall see some day our deliverance. Delivering the promise which was given by grace and was never a lie.

Civility

The many deaths should show that so many have gone before us. Let's put civil back into civilization. For death is always on our left shoulder. Let us find the comeback trail and form perfect relationships; our families come first and belong. So that we all can be healed and overflowing with grace. Where everyone is in righteous living, which comes from heaven above.

Righteousness

The gift of righteousness keeps us well in body and mind. Always given to us from grace. Receive the gift, for it belongs to all. No matter who you are, your birth was holy. You live to be holy; you came from holiness. So of course you can receive the gift of righteousness. It is yours; just ask. Your heavenly Father always loves you and is willing to give you righteousness.

Chapter 4
Dream

Permanence

Joy comes from heaven. The world does not give it, and the world cannot take it away. With self-control comes peace; with love comes great joy, and with generosity comes more joy. May the joy of the Lord always be with you.

You Be You.

Today you are you. That's truer than true. There is no one alive who is you and also no more than you. You are you. Just be you, for you are who you are. You be you. You're nothing but you. So be you. Thank you for being you.

Heaven Itself

Angels do sing on a holy pedestal. Love does reign among the constant atmosphere; peace is finally here in its place. All belong to the same spirit. All exist in a never-ending beauty. Constant is the perfect life among them and in them. All discover the awesome serenity which comes from their wonderful souls.

Christmas Now

In the morning one early December, birth was given for our salvation. Mother Mary kept the baby boy protected in her arms for the world. Finally had a savior as we pondered this miracle. May we all see Christmas within eternal light. Giving us divine hope to our precious lives.

Stars

Through it all, especially the hard times, my scars are shown, and they now are my stars. They dwell with me and are not concealed but shown from a humble beginning to now, a fervent present tense. Belonging to me and me alone. To never to be any more than what has happened and shown to all for how it was.

Newness

The attraction has always been where does it becomes a need. Even your beauty is very special. It may have always been conceived. Beginning to the end, your voice keeps me listening. Make it all happen, for you are complete and awesome. I may not be totally satisfied. It never does matter. For you are a creation which I admire and will flatter.

Perfection

Born as a child delivered in grace. Created by God and formed in his image. What can be more perfect than this? You are true. Truer than true. From the tip of your head to the bottom of your feet. Believe that you already have arrived and belong. For you are a spirit-led creation born for good.

A Solace Prayer

Lord, I do not know what to do. So I turn my face toward you. You become my essence. I become fluid like water flowing in a stream. No answers, no questions. The solutions just appear, and I do hear your voice above all things, coming in clear. Softly guiding me towards the divine.

Fear Not

Fear is like a jaguar which wants to crush your skull. It may pass. Only when you change your mind perpetuating a solid ground. Keeps us from falling and being fooled once more. Try and see the good; try and feel a different emotion. Maybe we can or cannot. But our peace can never be forgotten. For we never lose the love. We never leave those we love, and love remains in us.

Insist

Do you know? Can it be? Your attitude prevails. Only above mine when you curtail my passive mind and then we see to agree on only what you have said. And my mind does not matter. Only to become an invisible dread in the end, I wish it was not said.

Care

The love given from the heart. Only seems to hurt who I am. Even though I see you. My heart cannot and still loves beyond the soul divided. Comes the spirit of love that remains and in this void of help. Lasts a care for me and others out of love from heart.

Solemn Vow

He will take care of you. Your breath shines the lights. Amongst the stars fully bright. You exist no matter the occasion; slowly the heart beats. Bringing the transform nation. We are all together taken care of. Knowing that we have become much more than what we ought to be. Even though the struggle seemed for naught.

To Carry

Let your weight upon me and, I can carry you, no matter how heavy, for I love who you be. Who my brother I will stay. To make amends I always pray and hold you if I may. For the end is always the same; no matter you or me, the destination is always clear, so I will carry you ever so near.

Dream Again

What's true is always, even when hidden. Imagine again the reality which is truth. The true self will always become. It is seen within as well, good and fresh and eventually seen by all eyes that look. Look upon the experience that was given and see, for even the blind knows truth.
The truth will always set you free.

Chapter 5
Religion

A Religion

We all have a religion, no matter who you are. We all are part of the divine, whether you believe it or not. We are one. Together we make a difference. The world is not our eternal home; we belong for a while. And peacefully move on, becoming glorified into a new realm. Believe and you can see. Never again becoming one that is blind.

Holy Spirit

Aging concept battles. Thought in peace is an open space. Over the horizon our souls wait. Spirit contains all. All was created for good. Being part of the whole. Wholeness makes for a spirit awakening. Life to be blessed not condemned. We are immortal, playing a part and being consoled as we do wait.

Forgiving Self

Let love in; erase condemning thoughts so you can be a loving person. Accept yourself and others. Love does combat hatred and will always win. Love is the answer for forgiveness and grace. You are not your own. You were bought at a price. Created to be your real self, to claim a heavenly treasure given by grace. You are what you are, a holy person created by a holy God.

Jesus Letter

I know you are busy. I know you love me. I know you're for me; thank you, Jesus. I believe you can do anything. You have been with me. Sorry that I sometimes ignore you. I am not a perfect child. I try to remember my goodness. Even though I am not always good. Thank you, Jesus. I did confess my sins. I believe you forgot all of them. Remind me, Jesus, of your goodness. So I can forget my sins also. Thank you, Jesus.

The World

The world is not safe; many people in some kind of power grab cannot trust everyone, because you never know what goes on behind closed doors. I do esteem to help others though. Try and meet everyone where they're at. Being loving and kind, for my intimacy is private and my appetites are the same as anyone else.

As We Forgive

There is forgiveness of sins. You must forgive. You are forgiven. You must forgive yourself and others. Then God will forgive you. It is all about forgiveness. Sin does not reign when there is forgiveness, and love does conquer all evil. For God is merciful and wants you to show mercy.

I Am Forgiven.

Totally forgiven, much has been blessed. The proof is in spirit kindness and mercy holy was life, that was given much gratitude. Home is complete; the now is all. It is what matters from moment to moment is the sacred life. So now complete, much was done. All accepted, no worries now. Anger, anxiety, and stress, many known enemies, may attack for a while. Time shall defeat them; everything was good. Much was learned from adversity to peace, and peace became salvation.

God's Love

In the belief of a good God will help you understand that us creatures are immeasurably and totally loved. In prayer, beyond our thought processes, we find that love. The love God does gives us has always been and is eternal.

Saved

We are sealed and will be delivered. Love does save us. Freedom comes from the truth. The truth of the holy spirit. We shall be set free and given a mission by our heavenly Father. To be born into an everlasting life of love.

Inheritance

The grace, miracles, devotion from God really is not deserved; we deserved only to be guilty. But God's invaluable mercy does not condemn us. We are not condemned by God but only by ourselves. But instead, we are given an inheritance an inheritance by believing will never fade away.

Confidence

Your thought is the beginning of your active life. If you doubt in any way, you will not complete your destiny. Believe that you can. Do not fear; then you will. Today's impossibilities are tomorrow's victories. This ongoing life is yours and given by a good God.

The Dark

Some people do not like the light. They dwell in the darkness. Only hating those of the light. The one who is doing right. They always end up gone. Those in dark. After they complete their evil. When the sorrow has been done. They march onward further into the darkness.
Never to be seen again.

A Process

Life evolves. More than maybe now.
Some has past and going on.
May not last. Begun to fight. But will surrender.
Shall end for now; remember all
must go. The present is.
My past is gone. Death is final. Hope
does endure. Love will save.

Acknowledgements

Many thanks go out to my bowling partners from Parkway Bowl, especially Pete Franke, Wayne King and family. The many poems in this book were saved and given to me from them for reproduction.

Much gratitude for my wife and children who are an inspiration to me.

Finally, Jesus Christ and the Holy Spirit who helped tremendously.

Thanks again to all.

— Eugene Kaelin

www.ingramcontent.com/pod-product-compliance
Lightning Source LLC
LaVergne TN
LVHW010437070526
838199LV00066B/6054